MARK YOUNG

Melancholy

SurVision Books

First published in 2024 by
SurVision Books
Dublin, Ireland
Reggio di Calabria, Italy
www.survisionmagazine.com

Copyright © Mark Young, 2024

Cover image: "The Blue Bull Lost" by Victoria Chernyakhivska
© Victoria Chernyakhivska, 2024

Design © SurVision Books, 2024

ISBN: 978-1-912963-50-8

This book is in copyright. No part of this publication may be reproduced, stored in a retrieval system, or transmitted in any form or by any means without the prior permission in writing from the publisher.

Acknowledgements

Grateful acknowledgement is made to the editors of the following, in which some of these poems, or versions of them, originally appeared:

Alien Buddha, Argotist Online Poetry, Arteidolia, Fixator Press, Half Day Moon Journal, Ink Pantry, Lothlorien Poetry Journal, Misfitmagazine, Mobius: The Journal of Social Change, Moss Trill, otata, The Prairie Review, #Ranger, RIC Journal, Scud, Setu, SULΦUR Surrealist Jungle, Synchronized Chaos, Utsanga.it, and *Ygdrasil.*

CONTENTS

multistory temperance	5
despite which	6
looking over the overlooked	7
A quantum state	8
parrot raptor	10
It needs to keep lubricated to run properly	11
Strange, dear, but	12
The conspiracy fairy left me a silver dollar for my tooth	14
Being in sync with your alter ego	15
Corpuscular homunculi	16
Anna / Karenina is / back in town	17
Some organizations may be / eligible for tax deductible donations	18
Offworld peristalsis	19
The calliope	20
Fleshy condiments	21
Installing the new wi-fi extender	22
Indentured autodidacts	23
Nightingale	24
Adipose interventions	25
Melancholy	26
canvas asteroids	27
Ersatz in the 21st Century	28
Contextual petunias	29
our young have come to a final close	30
The fix is in	31
Target	32
A line from Aristotle	33
The Impresarios of Light	34
the tenth word	35

multistory temperance

Before diving deeper into the details, the images need to be further manipulated. There is only a limited amount of space; which means the entry must be vertical or nearly so. So many sites to explore. A linguistic search engine may be of help – though downward terminations need to extend a minimum of 100mm or else engage a void that uses its slope to trim the items correctly. That still means a lot of space will get used on your iPhone; & even though NASA says it's probably just space junk, it's surprising how much the dissolution of N2 in the blood acts as a space saver.

despite which

Cardamom seedpods lie across the
road leading out of the petrified
forest. The trains have stopped
running; & small birds are now
the carriers of freight, employed

to take away any detritus of em-
pire that still remains. Back into
the forest, following any one of
several flight paths that weave a
way through trunks & branches

that lead in many directions. Then
they disappear from sight – &
that is the last time the relics are
ever seen. But some hours later
the birds reappear, flying down

the road, each with a seedpod in
their beak which is dropped onto
the road below as they emerge out
into the open. Obviously payment
for their task, but from & for whom?

looking over the overlooked

The American frontier has lots of scenic views along the road from New York to Vladivostok including photocatalytic transformation of organic contaminants & other words you need to know. We are aware that viral infections have plagued humanity since time began, stemming partially from a refusal to believe that autism looks different in girls, & partially from the fact that many features often fail to load due to internet connectivity problems. Now, adrift in a plethora of postcolonial studies, we find ourselves forced to determine just what is the evidence behind the viral story linking gas stoves & the gothic in literature.

A quantum state

plays a powerful role in how we hear harmonies
is buying a VIP package at $1,249.99 for the upcoming Taylor Swift tour
demonstrates what black bears have to teach us about intelligence
is a mathematical entity that embodies the knowledge of a quantum system

suddenly does something completely different from what it was doing before
starts working in a 'happy ending' massage parlor on a three month contract
offers the most effective personalized fitness programs that are built with love
represents uncertainty about the real physical state of the system

considers *Eyes on the Prize* to be the finest documentary film series ever produced
tells the story of all the animals in the jungle holding an annual dance
is thinking of splurging on a lapdance the next time round
changes by a different set of rules than classical states

always wants to break away from the peleton
is less Schrödinger in *Papillon*, more Schroeder in *Peanuts*
is very rarely mistaken for an Australian or any other variety of
                                                         pelican
can be an eigenvector of an observable

makes its living by guest speaking on the restless nature of life
once crossed the Himalayas on a single-wheel mountain bike
is seriously considering gender reassignment surgery
is any possible state in which a quantum mechanical system can be

parrot raptor

Anagrammatic. Nominated for an Oscar. Reasonably well made with an ok price but the geometry on the fixed jaw could be modified to hold better. Also would provide a harmonious facial profile – is about proportion, not perfection. From each other, however, an attempt to establish a universal law, a categorical imperative. Calling up Kant, calling him out. Parroting his thoughts. Rapt or rapture?

It needs to keep lubricated to run properly

The side courtyard has only two entrances.
It was weird being on this side of the glass.
Royals enter the room in a specific order.

In the wild, most lobsters are a mottled greenish brown.
A Monday morning without coffee would be unthinkable.
I don't carry bananas around while I'm shopping.

You choose a premise or question & answer it yourself.
Nobody wants to be bitten by a snake.
I think it's fine, but out of curiosity what did they use?

Some BigTech firms have grown rapidly in the past decade.
Take this medication by mouth with or without food.
Camera Tamper rules can only be added or deleted.

Japanese text emoticons often give you a sore back.
Today was a start your car moment!
Exposure is particularly high among women & children.

Strange, dear, but

true, dear. The Cole Porter song enters
my morning mind as if it had every
right to be there, as if it lived there &
was returning home after a night out.
But not simply the song, a specific rend-
ition of it. k.d. lang's, first heard on the
Red Hot + Blue tv special & subsequent
album compilation. What is stranger is

how to interpret the locus of the singer,
of the mindsong. In the video, k.d. lang
sings as if she is person who is being
sung to; & in my mind, it is also as if I
am the recipient. To personalize, it is the
not-I singing to the other which is me. It's
a tableau that has a logic only because
of its similarity to that Magritte painting

La reproduction interdite in which a man is looking into a mirror in which his reflection is thrown back, but as if seen from the back. Twenty years ago I wrote of this painting: "Shown from the back the image is androgynous – think k.d. lang in her man's suit phase." & here she is again. Strange, dear, but true, dear.

The conspiracy fairy left me a silver dollar for my tooth

Jerry Fletcher is a man in love with a woman he observes from afar. Whoopi Goldberg questioned the Moon Landing on "The View." Jesse Ventura & his team of experts examine some of the most frightening & mysterious conspiracy allegations of contrails, which consist of ice crystals or water vapor condensed behind aircraft. Any gap in official information on such violent events is filled by online theorists proffering a "big explanation." Hoaxes go viral because the public rarely makes the distinction between conspiracy and misinformation in the aftermath of tragedy.

Secret schemes that shaped the world around us are hiding in the footnotes of our history books—you just need to know where to look. Urbandictionary.com is being used for governmental purposes. The government is finding out ways to control us, through an event or set of circumstances created as the result of a usually secret plot by powerful conspirators. Secretary Wolf calls these rumors "full of misstatements & misapprehensions."

The ads in this column are not endorsed by the author.

Being in sync with your alter ego

Allergic reactions to vaccines are very rare. They can also suggest ways to communicate more easily. Some titles will expire 48 hours after you first

press play. There are a number of signals that we can use if our feelings don't fit with our words. Use nonverbal signals when conversing with others.

A convenient abstraction is to model the value of a physical variable of interest by a number. In extreme cases allow customers to opt-in for text messaging.

Corpuscular homunculi

Reconstituted energy leaves sweat
stains on the sidewalk. Nothing else
dances like that, except, occasionally,
a presidential page when Air Force
One is targeted by voodoo bombs.

*

A zygote provides pro bono legal
work for a group of destitute ship-
ping containers who are currently
living in an old schoolhouse by the
river. It sings for its supper only
when naan bread is on the table.

*

A giant gerbil floats down from
the spires of the resident gothic cat-
hedral, looks up at the sun, & says:
"It must be atropine. Nothing else
could make the obelisk beat so fast."

Anna / Karenina is / back in town

Absolute targets have been shelved. The
perception of independence is now seen
as less vital than the ambiguous 'gray zone'
of subversive statecraft. Whatever apologies
are forthcoming resemble pre-shot videos,
& stand as testament to the outrage of an
influential section of the media who wanted
charges brought against the clergy as well

as the military. Any evidence offered has
been so heavily redacted it looks like a
blacked out *War & Peace*. All we need now
is Frank O'Hara to stand up at the U.N., bang
his shoe on the bench in front of him, & cry
out "Napoleon is coming on the right day."

Some organizations may be / eligible for tax deductible donations

Using empirical evidence & an
infinite lattice, the doctor, during
any process of obtaining diagno-
stic information, may stroke some
muscles to imitate the sounds of
a magnetic resonance imaging
investigation. It's a method – if
electronic networks are deemed
to be lacking – of conceptualizing
expressed behavior through faded
& forgotten artifacts. Escape peaks
are small; but just before escape,
a symmetry. The phase portrait
indicates only bounded solutions,
so an ancillary display of stone tools
has been put together as a physical
reminder of its strong connection
to the things we say to ourselves
but not to others. Something is be-
ing warmed inside a rice cooker
which, purportedly, is made from the
finest quality silicon carbide stone.

Offworld peristalsis

Men's design is happening faster than
at any other time in short-term memory.

Everything in heaps, spilling out every-
where, a series of muscle contractions.

Genre: Drum & Bass. Musicians: Robots
designed to emulate the locomotion of

worms. Most efficient response: Open a
CMD prompt as administrator & execute

any relevant command. Usual outcome: A
black buildup in pipes. Poor water flow.

The calliope

comes down the gang-
plank of the riverboat,
boasting to the waiting
reporters that she considers
herself to be the inventor
of steampunk – or, at

least, the precursor there-
of. Then she goes striding
through the lanes of Lon-
don, combat boots at the
ready, pipes pierced with
tethering rings or else en-

closed within vambraces,
shouting at anyone that
dares get in her way. All
the signs of being raised
as per the ABC of this type
of life – anal, banal, canal.

Fleshy condiments

A good hair accessory, on a bad hair day, is a powerful antioxidant that benefits your skin, immune system, & heart health. But do you know what flavorings should go with it? There are those relishes & sauces that your parents swore by to spice up the simplest scrunchie.

Or, if you're following a strict meat / hair regime, then maybe go for low-carb combs & bows. My fallback position is, regardless of the styling method, always season it with good serving of a yakiniku dipping sauce.

Installing the new wi-fi extender

Start the new year right – remove
any redundancy from your sent-
ences. Then move away from web-
based video channels that thrive on

a huge amount of laughable material
concerning cats & FAILS. Speak at
great length on the college hockey
team. Choose meaningful words &

be specific with your content. Give
listeners a Δ-regular graph G with n
vertices, & then segue into the most
recent version of the periodic table.

Indentured autodidacts

She does not write about what she does within a fractious world with a growing potential for conflict. Bodily autonomy is always a complex issue for any aspiring writer who, in a kind of morbid squirm, describes themselves

as being of an indeterminate class lost somewhere inside a ragged construct of fragile environments. The woeful uncertainty of her life needs a platform where playful public appearances are par for the course. Instead, as negoti-

ations for who alone will be the one to return the dead to life enter their final stages, she finds herself in a room in the house of a Boston candlemaker with no instructions on how to activate the myriad sconces that decorate its walls.

Nightingale

She's unlocked the center of gravity cheat in order to deal with the powerlimits found in the early stages of any affordable housing model. It demonstrates a new approach to building procurement. Now she's set out to decarbonize all of its built assets including a bookshelf that holds some reading material & multi-wear accessories, but is mainly lined with jars full of the yellow-orange flesh of persimmons. Is she acting differently to her usual daily routine? Hard to tell when she refuses to unlock the door.

Adipose interventions

Cellular senescence & the
impact of energy expenditure
can often be observed walking
hand in hand down the main
street of any circus town.

They're dressed in clown suits,
inhabit a liminal space between
the fantastic & the mundane
which they enter after the lions
but before the elephants. Some

passers-by say they fit well together; others that they look as
if they feed on one another. A
greater lifespan is often associated with a confounding effect.

Melancholy

"I used to think that relativity could be described as the last sausage left under the grill," they said to me as we shared a beer. "You know, the relatives have been around & eaten us out of house & home."

"Then I came across the *oeuvre* of de Chirico, & realized it had more to do with whether there were clocks in the painting, & were they larger than the artichokes or the enigmatic people they shared the space with."

canvas asteroids

In the prosaic sense that things
just work, find the ordinal of a
number using some black magic
& lots of glitter. Once that is done,
use screws of varying sizes to add
the back to the seat of the trephin-
ation machine. Putting a hole in
the head might seem quite easy
& straightforward when coded
from scratch, but getting the colors
right is a complex task. The moon
might arrive upside down before
the job is finished & draw the light
away. Sometimes it is the vibrations
from a herd of wombats digging
holes that causes the drill to slip.

Ersatz in the 21st Century

Newspapers can crumble into fragile
yellowed fragments. None of them
are palpable, except for a delicious
kind of fruit pie which can appear on
the menu at any time. Material goods
don't just disappear. Waste production
& management impact the oxymoron
that the concept of social nature turns

out to be. The Colorado River slowly
removes rocks to form a sector crucial
for trading goods & services but one
which ignores the welfare of performing
animals, the Grand Canyon, the adverse
effects of the phantasmagoric world.

Contextual petunias

Scientific research demonstrates that
even when amplified from trichomes &
scribed with random primers, paintball
with augurs often promises more than
it delivers. Done up in absolute-value
bars instead of square brackets, a 2 x 2
matrix may explain why this is the case
just as edited & blurred versions of drone

footage can reveal that gender is not just
a social construct nor one of the five most
popular horror movies of all time. Some
of these actions will be detrimental to the
psyche unless tempered with a desire that
blooms nonstop, no deadheading required.

our young have come to a final close

Phylogenetic under-
pinning used to be
buzz words in some
marginalized comm-

unities as a meta-term
to resolve the differences
between the mechanisms
involved in calculating

the cash discount rate
& coming to an under-
standing of the need
for bacterial pathogens.

The fix is in

Any attempt to cast
a wide conceptual
frame around the
cultural purpose &
historical dimensions
of the Hot Pink
Patent Point Toe
Square Stud Heel

Pumps Size 8
in the Clothing,
Shoes & Accessories
category on eBay is
almost certainly
motivated by politics.

Target

Temporal distortion. The breadth
of it. One side so far away
it cannot be seen, at least
not until some time has passed.
& even then, the numbers blur
as they are counted down.

*

Temporary distraction. The breaths
of it. Undecided cypher, a way
to cancel out the scene, to lease
the space under some half passage
& eventually, as numbness slurs
the speech's cadences, die out.

A line from Aristotle

According to either
Rolling Stone or *Harper's
BAZAAR,* dance is
partly a visual aesthetic

& partly conceptual, an
art won by training &
habituation. But that
doesn't explain why

polymath book editors
don't seem to favor
al fresco jiving, even
when there are savings

to be made by using
coupons. Something
about the cinnamon
is not quite right.

The Impresarios of Light

arrive in darkness. Those who
are surprised by this bat it away
by saying it's a way to heighten
the contrast. Others, with more
extreme views, ascribe it to the
influence of those game-playing
wikis which elevate the eldritch
to a necessary component of any
form of fine art. The impresarios
emerge smiling at all the misinter-
pretations, do not seek to remind
the mind-blind crowd that darkness
always travels at the speed of light.

the tenth word

The theater is a place of queuing dictators, whose claque stands in a broken bamboo balcony, surrounded by barbed wire & the O of a singing mouth. Mimicking some radical equation, a bus leaves the nearby corner carrying a splinter group. Shiva lingering. Bleached membranes, inverted summer machinery. Long supple typewriters run wild under the dome.

Selected Poetry Titles Published by SurVision Books

Contemporary Tangential Surrealist Poetry: An Anthology
Edited by Tony Kitt
ISBN 978-1-912963-44-7

Invasion: An Anthology of Ukrainian Poetry about the War
Edited by Tony Kitt
ISBN 978-1-912963-32-4

Helen Ivory. *Maps of the Abandoned City*
(New Poetics: England)
ISBN 978-1-912963-04-1

Tony Kitt. *The Magic Phlute*
(New Poetics: Ireland)
ISBN 978-1-912963-08-9

John Bradley. *Spontaneous Mummification*
(Winner of James Tate Poetry Prize 2019)
ISBN 978-1-912963-13-3

Dominique Hecq. *Endgame with No Ending*
(Winner of James Tate Poetry Prize 2022)
ISBN 978-1-912963-42-3

J V Birch. *ice cream 'n' tar*
(Winner of James Tate Poetry Prize 2022)
ISBN 978-1-912963-43-0

James Cyphers Wright. *Fuel for Love*
(Winner of James Tate Poetry Prize 2023)
ISBN 978-1-912963-45-4

Order our books from http://survisionmagazine.com

www.ingramcontent.com/pod-product-compliance
Lightning Source LLC
Chambersburg PA
CBHW061313040426
42444CB00010B/2618